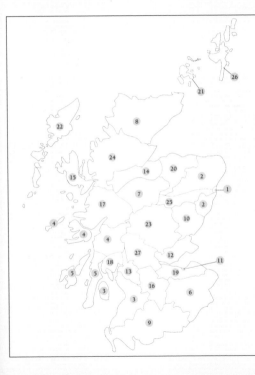

1. Aberdeen
2. Aberdeenshire
3. Arran & Ayrshire
4. Northern Argyll
5. Southern Argyll
6. The Borders
7. The Cairngorms
8. Caithness & Sutherland
9. Dumfries and Galloway
10. Dundee & Angus
11. Edinburgh
12. Fife, Kinross & Clackmannan
13. Glasgow
14. Inverness

15. The Isle of Skye
16. Lanarkshire
17. Lochaber
18. Loch Lomond, Cowal & Bute
19. The Lothians
20. Moray
21. Orkney
22. The Outer Hebrides
23. Perthshire
24. Ross & Cromarty
25. Royal Deeside
26. Shetland
27. Stirling & The Trossachs

The remaining two books, Distinguished Distilleries and Scotland's Mountains, feature locations throughout the country so are not included in the above list.

Colin Nutt

PICTURING SCOTLAND

INVERNESS

NESS PUBLISHING

2   The mouth of the River Ness viewed from Kessock Bridge.

INVERNESS

Welcome to Inverness! Fàilte gu Inbhir Nis!

Granted city status in 2000, Inverness (Inbhir Nis in Gaelic) has been known as the Capital of the Highlands for many years. Situated at the north-eastern end of the Great Glen and on the Moray Firth, it is a natural route centre that also provided early settlers with a choice of secure elevated sites on which to live. One of these is the hill fort of Craig Phadraig, on the western side of Inverness. This is believed to be where St Columba met the Pictish King Brude, introducing him to Christianity in approximately 565AD. A later hilltop castle to the east of the city is said by some to be where Macbeth murdered King Duncan I in 1040.

In more civilised vein, around 1150 King David I granted charters that gave Inverness royal burgh status. This privilege stimulated the development of the town, but in the troubled Middle Ages its growing importance made it a target for vying factions in the endless strife of that era. Inverness went through a cycle of prosperity and destruction (usually by being burnt), often as a result of royalty's attempts to bring unruly Highland clans into line. For example, Clan Donald burned the town at least seven times. The tensions between regional chiefs and the monarchy are also seen in the visit of Mary, Queen of Scots, to Inverness in 1562. The castle's governor, Alexander Gordon, refused her entry to the fortress which resulted in a siege. Once the castle was taken, Gordon was hanged.

Looking north from Inverness Castle with Ben Wyvis in the distance. **5**

6   Inverness from the air looking north-west, with the River Ness winding its way through the city. The expanse of sea at top right is the Moray Firth.

Early industries included fishing and shipbuilding while the main exports through the port were wool, fur and hides. Later, brewing and whisky distilling developed. A foundry was established in 1872. Some of its work can still be seen in the suspension bridges that cross the River Ness in the city.

The River Ness defines the city, its name meaning 'mouth of the Ness'. The classic views of the city all feature the river, often including the notable buildings on either side. The river begins at the northern end of Loch Ness and for a short distance doubles as part of the Caledonian Canal. This famous waterway, built by Thomas Telford, opened in 1822. The last few miles of the canal diverge from the river and curve their way around the western side of Inverness, finally meeting the sea (in the form of the Beauly Firth) at Clachnaharry, a north-western suburb.

The first railway from Inverness opened in 1855, initially as far as Nairn. When in later

Kessock Bridge.

8   The mountains west of Inverness are barely noticeable in summer, but add a layer of snow and view through a long lens and the city's backdrop is transformed. The picture was taken from Alturlie on

the Moray Firth just east of Inverness. The mountain is Sgurr na Lapaich (1150m/3773ft) which is about 35 miles distant, so even in the clear winter air it has a slightly soft-focus look to it.

9

10 Gerald Laing's statue in Falcon Square with detail of unicorn, right

years connections went right through to England, a tourism boom resulted. Today's rail network still takes travellers over to the west coast at Kyle of Lochalsh, to the far north with termini at Thurso and Wick and eastwards through to Aberdeen, as well as the main route south to Edinburgh, Glasgow and England.

This book aims to show how the area's blend of towns and villages, mountains and lochs, rivers and firths, provides a feast of cultural and visual treats for all who come to explore the region.

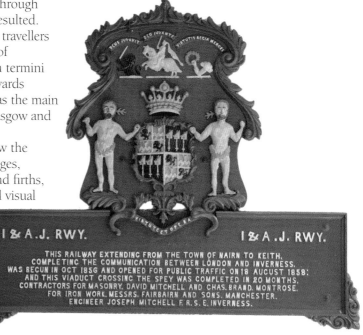

Commemorative plaque at Inverness station. 11

12 Inverness city centre as seen from Friars Bridge.

Looking across the River Ness from Huntly Street towards Douglas Row. **13**

14 St Stephen's, The Old High Kirk, is the oldest building in Inverness, part of which dates back to the 14th century.

Free North Church from Greig Street Bridge.

The castle through spring foliage.

16 Inverness Castle, built from 1833 to 1836. Today it serves various purposes including that of High Court for the Highland Region.

Close-up of Inverness Castle with a statue of Flora Macdonald in the foreground.

18 St Andrew's Cathedral, situated by Ness Walk and built from 1866 to 1869.

Interior of St Andrew's: the high altar, left, and the font, right. **19**

20   Inverness Castle floodlit at Christmas.

A little further up the River Ness, this view looks across to some of the Ness Bank restaurants. **21**

22 Autumn in Inverness, with the towers of St Andrew's Cathedral visible above the trees.

By contrast, the spring flowers and blossoms are at their best at Cavell Gardens which provide a 23 lovely setting for the War Memorial on Ness Bank.

24 The same gardens seen in summer guise, looking across the River Ness towards the Royal Northern Infirmary.

26 Eden Court Theatre on Bishop's Road, pictured around the time of its re-opening following a multi-million pound redevelopment.

More recently, these decorative embellishments have been added to the theatre's grounds. **27**
The theatre's reflection can be made out in the stainless-steel spheres.

28 Bellfield Park, on Island Bank Road. Open air concerts are given at the park's bandstand during summer.

Looking downstream towards St Andrew's Cathedral with Ord Hill behind. **29**

30 Left: riverside villas at Lady's Walk on Ness Bank. Right: looking back across the river from in front of those same houses, a fly-fishing demonstration – this is a popular anglers' beat.

The Ness Islands add interest to the river upstream from here. A footpath winds its way through the islands and across the river, allowing a circular walk.

32 Left: the Alexander Dunbar Infirmary, dated 1668, in Church Street. The plaque on p.4 is on this building. Right: Abertarff House, built 1593 and also in Church Street, is the oldest secular building in Inverness.

Balnain House, built 1726, left, and a former church building, on Huntly Street. **33**

34 Two imposing buildings on Bridge Street: the Town House, completed in 1882, left, opposite which is the former Bank of Scotland building, now the Caledonian bar.

Interior of the Victorian Market and one of its more traditional shop fronts. The market lies within **35** the rectangle formed by Academy Street, Union Street, Church Street and Queensgate.

36 Looking down Eastgate from St Stephen's Brae.

Inverness Museum and Art Gallery, with the Tolbooth Steeple of 1791 to its right. **37**

38 Muirtown locks on the Caledonian Canal. The Canal opened in 1822 linking Inverness with Fort William at the other end of the Great Glen.

The canal basin at Muirtown.

40 The hilly western suburbs of Inverness pictured from North Kessock. The picture on the next page was taken from near the top of this hill …

42 ... looking down from the north side of which gives this view down to the Beauly Firth.

After passing through Inverness the Caledonian Canal reaches the sea at Clachnaharry **43** through one last lock.

44 The Kessock Bridge, opened in 1982, links Inverness with the Black Isle, carrying the A9 to the far north.

In the South Kessock district of Inverness, a finely carved 'Nessie' looks across to the village of **45** North Kessock, which was connected to Inverness by ferry until the bridge was built.

46 The Kessock Bridge is worth walking over to take in scenes like this. From the northern approaches, this is the westerly view over the Beauly Firth.

By the shores of Loch Dochfour (the stretch of water between Loch Ness and the River Ness), **47** rhododendrons in full flower make a fine sight in this loch-side estate.

48 We now begin a south-west to north-east journey to take a look at the region around Inverness. This begins in Fort Augustus at the southern end of Loch Ness, through which the Caledonian Canal passes

The luxury cruise vessel *Lord of the Glens* squeezes through the locks at Fort Augustus. **49**
This 54-passenger ship cruises extensively around the west coast of Scotland.

50 The hills around Loch Ness hide many other smaller lochs, in exquisite settings. This is Loch Tarff, tucked away in the hills on the southern side of Loch Ness, not far from Fort Augustus.

Urquhart Castle is imposingly situated on the shores of Loch Ness near the village of Drumnadrochit. **51**
Its origins as a fortress possibly go back to the Iron Age.

52 Urquhart Castle Keep. One of Scotland's largest castles, it was reduced to ruins in 1692 to prevent the Jacobites from using it.

Rainbow over Urquhart Castle. A legend relates that St Columba encountered the **53** Loch Ness Monster here in the 6th century.

54 The *Jacobite Queen* leaves Urquhart Castle pier for another spell of monster spotting!

The Great Glen experiences temperature inversions quite often, mostly in spring or autumn, resulting **55** in thick mists like this. Meall Fuar-Mhonaidh (on the right) appears to be floating on the clouds.

56 Unusual light effects can sometimes appear over Loch Ness. The author has seen just this colouration on an occasion when it was not possible to take a photograph. This view, taken from near Dores at the

northern end of the loch, was similar and has been slightly tinted in an attempt to replicate the sight
once seen. Colour apart, it gives a good impression of the loch's 22-mile length.

58 Left: the Falls of Foyers, in the village of the same name on the south side of Loch Ness, form a spectacular sight with a drop of 49m/160ft. Right: the ravine of Foyers Glen drops steeply to Loch Ness.

The classic viewpoint for Loch Ness sunsets is at the village of Dores at the northern end of **59** the loch, by the Dores Inn.

60 Not far from Dores, up in the little-known district around Dunlichity, a pattern of lochs invites exploration. Here we see Loch Duntelchaig early on an autumn morning.

Close by is the smaller Loch a' Clachan, an absolute gem in its setting of craggy hills.

62 Now we go north of the Great Glen to the mountains around Glen Affric, about 30 miles south-west of Inverness and famed as being one of the most beautiful glens in Scotland.

Sgurr na Lapaich sits to the right of the previous picture, overlooking Glen Affric. **63**
Its challenging summit is inset.

64 Waterfall in Glen nam Fiadh, the next valley to the north of Glen Affric.

Further up Glen nam Fiadh presents this mountain view with Tom a Choinich in the **65** middle distance and Mam Sodhail in the far distance.

66 The next valley north again is Glen Cannich. In this winter-wonderland scene, the snow in the foreground has turned into ice crystals, giving it an amazingly sparkly appearance.

Glen Cannich's reservoir, Loch Mullardoch, lies frozen on its shadier side. This is a glen that is **67** missed by many, but its solitude adds to the enchantment for those who do come here.

68 An aerial view of Tomatin Distillery, near the village of the same name, about 15 miles south of Inverness. Distillery tours are available.

The attractive town of Beauly is situated about 12 miles west of Inverness. The town square, **69** seen here, is where a number of interesting features are located.

70 Beauly's origins go back to the founding of the Priory in 1230 by the Valliscaulian order, one of three they established in Scotland. The town grew up around it.

Another scene from Beauly. The character on the right may or may not put in an appearance
at the time of your visit to the town!

72 From the hill fort of Craig Phadraig on the outskirts of Inverness (it's the hill in the picture on p.40), this scene stretches away to the west along the Beauly Firth and to the hills beyond. The town of

Beauly lies just beyond the loch shore at the top right of the picture.

74 Main picture: Culloden Battlefield on the moors just east of Inverness is one of Scotland's most important historical sites. Inset: boggy terrain, not good for fighting.

A piper and 'soldier' at the annual service of remembrance at the commemorative cairn on the **75** battlefield. The one-sided battle of 16th April 1746 finally and brutally ended the Jacobite uprisings.

76 Leanach Cottage stands on the battlefield. Its last inhabitant, a Mrs MacDonald, left in 1912.

Some of the many grave markers at Culloden. The new visitor centre does an excellent job of explaining and interpreting the battle and its causes – do go there to discover the full story.

78 Early morning sun filters through the arches of Culloden railway viaduct as the morning train from Inverness to London gets into its stride.

Ancient remains are plentiful around Inverness: here, east of the city in the valley of the River Nairn, **79** are Clava Cairns, an extensive collection of Bronze Age standing stones and chambered cairns.

80 Left: an aerial view of Cawdor Castle, situated a few miles east of Culloden.
Right: The Drawing Room of Cawdor Castle.

Cawdor Castle dates from the late 14th century and was built as a private fortress by the **81** Thanes of Cawdor. It is open to the public from May to early October.

82 The Moray Firth is home to a great variety of marine life including Grey Seals …

… and Bottlenose Dolphins. Where they might appear is, of course, unpredictable; however the narrow stretch of the Firth between Fort George (see over) and Chanonry Point is a good prospect.

84 Fort George, on the Moray Firth near the village of Ardersier, was built to discourage further uprisings after Culloden. Pictured are the drawbridge and a rotating gun emplacement.

Fort George is one of the most outstanding fortifications in Europe, taking 21 years to build from **85** 1748 to 1769. This view shows the Guardroom block.

86 Fort George holds a number of historical re-enactment events each year. Here, a skirmish from the 17th-century Covenanter War is recreated with live musket fire adding realism.

Also at Fort George, but on a lighter note, these dancers show off their moves from a Second World War-era dance floor complete with Swing band.

88 This winter landscape was captured from Tomhommie, a hamlet between Ardersier and Nairn. The mountain in the background is Ben Wyvis (1045m/3428ft), about 25 miles away.

90 The final stop on this journey is the seaside town of Nairn. Left: the war memorial on Cawdor Road. Right: the beautifully crafted Fishwife statue on the seafront.

Nairn Museum specialises in local history, with artefacts and collections of local life, including this **91** reconstruction of a home from an earlier era. Well worth a visit!

92 Early morning in summer at Nairn Links, with the bandstand on the left. Inset: a close-up of the fine detailing on the bandstand.

The Links are also the venue for the annual Nairn Highland Games. Here, a caber is in mid-toss, under the watchful eyes of the adjudicators.

94 Nairn harbour in winter. Like Inverness, Nairn benefits from the Moray Firth micro-climate.

Nairn has an excellent and extensive beach. Perhaps it is no surprise that Nairn was once branded as **95** the 'Bournemouth of the North'. It is still an excellent place for a seaside holiday.

Published 2011 by Ness Publishing, 47 Academy Street, Elgin, Moray, IV30 1LR. Reprinted 2014.
Phone 01343 549663 www.nesspublishing.co.uk
(First edition published in 2008 entitled *Inverness: a pictorial souvenir*)

All photographs © Colin and Eithne Nutt except pp.6 & 68 © Scotavia Images; p.80 (both) © Cawdor Castle;
and pp.82 & 83 © Charlie Phillips; p.91 reproduced by permission of Nairn Museum

Text © Colin Nutt
ISBN 978-1-906549-31-2

Front cover: the River Ness and Inverness Castle; p.1: an Inverness cameo; p.4: detail from Alexander Dunbar House;
this page: Cromwell Tower (only surviving part of citadel); back cover: sunset over Loch Ness

For a list of websites and phone numbers please turn over > > > >

Websites and phone numbers (where available) in the order they appear in this book:

www.inverness-scotland.com
www.visithighlands.com
Train services: www.firstgroup.com/scotrail
Inverness Castle: www.castleuk.net
St Andrew's Cathedral: www.invernesscathedral.co.uk
Eden Court Theatre: www.eden-court.co.uk (T) 01463 234234
The Victorian Market: www.invernessvictorianmarket.co.uk
Inverness Museum & Art Gallery: www.invernessmuseum.com (T) 01463 237114
Loch Ness: www.lochnesswelcome.co.uk
Loch Ness Cruises: www.jacobite.co.uk (T) 01463 233999
Urquhart Castle: www.historic-scotland.gov.uk (T) 01456 450551
Caledonian Canal: www.scottishcanals.co.uk (T) 01463 725500
Tomatin Distillery: www.tomatin.com (T) 01463 248148
Beauly: www.visitbeauly.com
Beauly Priory: www.historic-scotland.gov.uk
Culloden Battlefield: www.nts.org.uk (T) 0844 493 2159
Clava Cairns: www.historic-scotland.gov.uk
Cawdor Castle: www.cawdorcastle.com (T) 01667 404401
Fort George: www.historic-scotland.gov.uk (T) 01667 460232
Nairn: www.nairnscotland.co.uk